THE BENCH

REBECCA TAKSEL

THE BENCH

REBECCA TAKSEL

MADBOOKS

2020

MadBooks
Pittsburgh, PA 15221

FIRST EDITION

ISBN: 978-0-9995521-4-8

I. Late Summer

Walking along a paved road in a country park
with my parents and my tiny brother—so long ago—
and the pavement ended,

gave way to grass,
acres of grass,
looming to the horizon,
full of wildflowers and
weeds and here and there a tree.

I asked my parents if this was the end
of all the streets,
all of them everywhere.
I was trying to ask if it was the end of the world.

I've come back to the end now, I think,
to listen to the silent wilderness,
to smell the silent grass.

This morning I left a plastic bag
under my bench in the park by the church.
Nothing much in it—
a container of breadcrumbs for the birds,
a pair of slippers,
my scarf with the sailboats on it.

When I came back to the bench
a woman was sitting there.
She saw me and moved to the far end
and crossed her legs
and pulled her jacket around her.

She won't talk to me.
If she gets bored and talks to me I'll hum.
She's all dressed up. She noticed
the gray plait coiled on my head,
and my old denim skirt
and my old tennis shoes
and my sweater with holes at the elbows
but it's a good sweater, she wouldn't know that.
So she won't talk to me
but if she does I'll hum.

Listen to the cicadas,
listen to the leaves
that fall and crackle on the path,
I could say to her.
I just say it to myself.

The bag is where I left it.
It's safe to leave things, the church is right here.
Three little holes have been eaten in the bag—
snails? a caterpillar?

and in the shrubbery by the church,
a beautiful cat,
black and white, with green eyes.

There are a lot of days when I sit for a long time on the bench. I can see my house from here. The best days are the ones that just happen because I'm not trying to make them into anything and I don't let thoughts pull me in any direction. Interruptions are usually OK, I just hum through them or I close my eyes and feel movements and disturbances in the air, nothing to be afraid of. Sometimes the kids fight but they don't come too close, only once or twice they yelled things at me but they could see I didn't have anything to take. My friend Miss Roxanne laughs at them or hollers at them to get on back to school and where are their mothers or grandmothers and what a shame and disgrace. She's right but I can't say that because I'm an old white lady and she's a black lady of an age I cannot figure out and wouldn't ask. She calls me Miss Margaret and I call her Miss Roxanne. She used to call me Miss Bailey but I told her to call me by my first name and that's where we've landed. She knows everybody in the neighborhood and that's how she knows my last name. She saw me coming out of 424 Lamar Street and she said Baileys been living in that house forever and was I a Bailey? She says the neighborhood went down now the neighborhood's coming up or that's what she's heard and what does it mean anyway? I close my eyes when she talks, not because I want to shut out her voice but so I can concentrate on it because it's so low and it sends out words like coated candies, like the ones at Gimbel's all those years ago, that seemed holy to me because you only saw them at Christmas.

I have no value, my currency is low. I know what I look like as I sit here. I never counted for much. I never had to count or be counted much. I didn't know how to spend what I had, I came home young and hoarded the little I had but not counting, just keeping something safe from the outside. Counting and numbers are exhausting and never end, there is always $n+1$. I don't remember much math beyond arithmetic but I always remembered that, and it caused me a depth of anguish I felt every time I pictured it on a page full of numbers and symbols. I stopped it, no plus-one, just me and I keep to myself.

Miss Roxanne, who is my friend and sits with me sometimes on the bench tells me that for her family everything had to be counted, every mouthful of food and every mile between Georgia and Pennsylvania. I sigh with her and travel with her silently along the road as she describes her grandparents driving the two-lane roads up through the South. I just sigh and listen and hear a dangerous country of red earth and dull pine rolling away under almost-worn-out tires. Miss Roxanne doesn't talk too much, just the right number of words. She makes each one of them round and flowing, bubbles over stones in a clean creek. I want to reach over and take her hand which is smoother than mine and two colors, the palm lighter, so I can feel the words traveling through her. But of course I don't. I will tell her about the street when it was all white people who were so sure they counted for a lot but made surer by passing sneaky laws to keep the colored people out. She already knows and she is not bothered about not counting. She sits up straight.

When I was young
I went away and kept coming back
then one day I stayed.
That is the simplest best way to tell myself my life
after all this time. I stayed because I wanted to be quiet.

The hum of music vibrates along my nerves and my dry lips.
This has been my quiet life for a long time.
Not like the lives I tried on, each one a necklace made of blades.
We were a peaceful family my mother my father my brother Joe

When I was a child
I felt myself torn apart by knives
when I walked out the door
I was scared of passing by certain boys dogs houses girls teachers,
then every month bleeding too young really the first one in my class
and I never said to Mother I was in pain and soaking with blood
I ran home blue skirt full of brown stains I wasn't even eleven

and had no idea where babies came from,
Mother said the Milky Way
which is beautiful to think about even now
human life descending from stars so thick in the sky
they swirl and foam and pour out drops and streams of life.

I remember being a child, being a pair of grave eyes,
the feelings gone, the smells and tastes of things.
I remember a little gray ghost with eyes.

Baltimore was the wildest of the young wild years I had.
Time and place we make our own, fused hot.

Valentine sings forever on a sticky July night at a bar in the harbor.
Her voice falls into the oily black water and emerges maybe thousands
of miles away on a little mound of sand and rock or is forever submerged
inside of me now here in the cold far away
but the time and the place remain.

Oil and sweat are on the ocean air, and heat that promises to lift away
any snow or ice that dares to touch the southern soul of this city.
Streets that slope to the water, you can sit or stand facing the ocean and eat
oysters forced open to reveal each one a whole ocean,
why not drink the ocean
or at least smell it with every breath?

There's another bar in the direct shadow of the prison right near
downtown
where black and white girl-women try each other out as soul mates,
reflections
through smudged wavy mirrors, nobody having words to describe what
they see
or the feel of oiled tight black curls under pale fingers and the delicate
smell of hair oil
and what is left to shine in the cradle of the oyster shell.

It is a torment and a blessing to sit with the animals and the birds. I don't see them as a tableau set out for my pleasure or my instruction. I'm afraid to feel too close to them. Some people can do that, enter into the lives of animals. My brother Joe could do that. When he was four he saw terror in the eye of a little brown rabbit on our lawn. It was the beginning of his life as a being who lived as an equal to everyone and everything around him. I say "around" but that makes him the center and he didn't see it that way. He was in the web of the world and he tugged lightly on the web in every direction. He taught me some of that, I suppose. I sit now maybe looking like a spider to the people walking through the park. A lot of people avoid me. But the crows and the cats and the squirrels and the sparrows don't see me that way, I'm sure. They move in patterns invisible to me except where we intersect. Their eyes are different, what they see. I know that.

I can't tell people not to sit on the bench.
This person has a phone with big numerals.
The kids or grandkids bought it for her.
She sits on the bench
as far from me as she can
the way most of them do
and holds her phone
in front of her face.
We used to hold books like that.

If someone friendly comes along
she'll point the phone at them.
Her fingers will slide slide slide
through a hundred pictures of the grandkids
--where's the one with . . . not that one . . . wait . . .

She'll spare me. She won't show them to me.
I won't have to shout at her
what I've seen all around
the bench in the park:
Cycles of life come in all forms,
some with claws, some with spots,
some with a million eyes, a million stars.

from far above dark water
I look down on the savage girl
flung out of heaven onto the beach
she was myself

knowing how she got there
crazy and stupid
almost to death

I watch the violence of her breath
run up and down
her naked back
a serpent under her skin

II. Fall

A few notes of jazz—New York
so long ago—
tumble through sunlight and dust
from an open window.
I am wrapped
in a beam of light and sound,
helpless, immortal,
caught in a slow spinning dance.

Shreds of brown bark,
brown leaves
on an unswept path,
crackle and shatter underfoot,
great drifts of leaves
twirl up from the path
like treasured pages
I forgot to read.
A slanting ray of sun,
long, dangerous,
finds me.

Finally, late, air like water,
green and glowing with sun,
water covering the street,
a sheen of gold.
The moment is permeable,
I can swim in air,
I can breathe in water.

Green and gold fade.
In a disheveled sky,
blue air trails tattered cloud,
thick white mist shrouds
the rising moon.

Father, mother, brother, in that order.
Father July 29, the day after Mother's birthday.
Years later: Mother, on the ninth of March
six months to the day after Joe's birthday.
More years later: Joe, January 25,
one month after Father's Christmas birthday.

I carry this puzzle of numbers around
the dates of death,
and I rearrange the pieces,
as if I believed in conjuring with them,
as if they were bones.
People used to do that.
I don't believe in it.
But the numbers fit in my mind,
in my hands almost,
polished, like bones

I see little bones in the grass or on the walks,
dropped by the owls,
left by the cats and the children,
or maybe the animal just died—
a little skeleton of a vole, perfect.
The bones are cleaned by teeth and rain and sun.
I could pick them up and shake them:
Where are my parents? Where is my brother?

We never traveled to Greece or Rome.
Granddad lost his money in the Depression.
We had prints on the wall,
Ruins of Greece and Rome.
I am a ruin, a body is a ruin,
a tumbled building, a gouged column.

The little gash in my knee from that picnic
when I was so young, the Hungarian ladies.
set a slab of fat bacon on a stick over a fire
and caught drippings on bread.
I drank homemade wine and I fell
and my knee bled
but I didn't feel it.
Other marks, too, they happen,
you are young, you don't mind.

But I was ruined young.
Rovinata. I remember the Italian word,
rovinata, a turning word. Being ruined in Italian
is like being turned on a rotisserie
and slowly burned. Yes.

Those years in college, the expensive one.
The boys or men—what were they?—
so strong and cruel they seemed like men.
I let them do whatever they wanted.
It wasn't much, almost always the same.
And there, in that place at the center
of myself I was ruined.
Now I can sit and walk and not mind
and feel the folds over the flesh
at the center of myself and feel it as part of myself,
it quickens to the beauties of the world around me,
all the things that fall on the path, feathers and acorns
and a fluttering blue scarf stolen from a lady
by the wind.

I remember a dress, gray-blue silk chiffon,
in my mother's closet,
waiting for an evening out,
brushing against plainer things.

Her perfume, Tweed,
an October perfume,
wood and earth and nutmeg,
I almost remember it, not quite,
just as well,
even a color, mist blue,
and the feather feel of the silk—

I remember them, though,
my mother and my father,
walking into the evening,
wrapped in their October
of mists and clouds and
perfume of dry leaves,
their anniversary month.

Dress, scent of earth,
footsteps on dry leaves,
quiet voices, man and woman—

a past too far past,
a past with no road, no map,
a black gulf of years.
A color, only.
A perfume, only.

Casement windows: old glass, black mullions,
set in a stone façade.
Blue awning, oak door,
everything small, discreet,
easy to miss on the busy New York street.

I looked through the windows,
knowing what I'd see:
tables set with white cloths and heavy silver,
carpet like thick moss underfoot
a tiny bar to the left,
Campari and *fino* sherry,
and a great bouquet of flowers wrapped in cellophane.

I think about that place.
I know what I will wear when I go there:
a plain gray suit
with a brooch in the shape of a cheetah,
a very fine black handbag fitted with a compact,
black gloves,
a hat, a little crescent of black feathers
whose tips will brush my cheek.

I will sit alone at the table by the window
with a cocktail in a fine stemmed glass.
I will watch drops of gin and vermouth
gather on the rim of the glass,
and I will let the drops fall,
one after another,
into a tiny stream on the base of the glass.

There must be a progress through life, a purifying. I must cut away, cut down, relinquish, let go. There are too many things. People are poisoned by a silting up of things around them, imprisoned by objects that were worthless the day they were made. I will not be distracted by people and their naming of things. I am alone, as I knew I was meant to be. I allow myself a few things in my house, the inlaid table, the beveled mirror, the good chairs, the maple dresser. Mementoes, only a few: mother's book, father's violin, brother's jacket. I had most of the things removed. There are men who come around; you have to pay them to take things away. Nothing worth selling in most houses. I saw the older moving man eyeing the things I told him to remove, calculating the prices he would get for them.

I must be shriven, sins confessed, lifted away so that I am light, light. I feel the house key in my pocket, nothing else.

My progress is to wear myself smooth, a stone, cleaned and polished by the pure salt sea. The ashes of my brother are not a fine smooth dust but a pebbly mix, a gravel studded with bone, purified by fire. You cannot live after immersion in fire, but you can be purified by water, and by the air on windy days: those gusts that tumble you around, flatten you against walls and benches, leaving you gasping—if the wind is cold enough you feel cleansed.

Every time a new policeman or policewoman is assigned to our neighborhood they have to see about me. I have to show the house key, sometimes I have to walk over to the house and show the policeman or the policewoman I can open the door. Sometimes they want to come in. I tried to stop the first one but after that I realized it's easier to go along with them. They come in the front room and see it's all right, no ceiling falling down and if it's winter it's not freezing. I don't talk to them, I hum while we walk over to the house and walk through it. Then I walk back out and they have to walk out too.

I go back to the park and then they leave me alone. It's a small place and usually peaceful. The church is over a hundred years old, gray stone, not large, solid, the plain Presbyterian church where we always went, so I feel at home. I don't go to services there anymore. I tried for a long time, but I realized no one was there anymore to hear my prayers.

I like to sit on the bench closest to the church in the park. If someone else is sitting on that bench, I take another one. The park is just grass and a few shrubs and trees. Enough shelter for the small animals. A few times there were deer. So terrible to see them in the city like that. They're all out of scale for the little park. The nearest woods are a couple of miles away. I prayed and prayed they would find their way back. I left the park and shut myself inside. Next day no deer, not alive or dead. I told myself they found their way back.

I see Joe on a bench in a park
maybe my park, I think so.
Sometimes he is the old man
he never became,
sometimes he is young, my little brother,
one arm flung along the top of the bench,
feet in running shoes
ankle crossed on opposite knee.

I want to come close and talk to him,
but I need words that are careful
and quiet, so he won't disappear.
I want words like thin breezes,
or like sun crazy with summer dust
from the garden path,
or golden and fluttering like ginkgo leaves.

I want words to speak in a whisper
to his sad eyes,
words that brush his cheek and fly away,.

I want to hold his calloused hands, lightly,
so I feel the pulses in his fingers.
Can I do this?
Or will I wake up sobbing,
his image exploded,
his death a swirl of loud screaming winds?

III. Winter

I will have to go inside for these months.
I wish the cats could come inside.
I don't worry about the squirrels.
I worry about Jack, who is homeless.
Will he go to the shelter? Will he blow away
with the last leaves and come back next spring?

I have a house. Lamar Street.
The house where we all lived,
four-twenty-four Lamar,
I had to give the address to the policeman again,
it's getting hard to talk with my outside voice.
He took me home. He thought maybe I was lying.
But I told him I had my own house,
a good house.

I stay on the first floor now:
kitchen, other room used to be the dining room,
other room closed up used to be the parlor,
little bathroom, bigger bathroom upstairs.
Furnace is good, I pay the bills
but not telephone I don't bother with the telephone.
I told him that when he brought me home.
I used my key in the door and he went away
and my outside voice quieted down.

Some day this winter,
when the sky is clear and high
and cold white sunlight finds its way
through the front window,
I will climb up to the attic.

I will be careful.
The house is haunted
by my memories.
The room in the attic, big roses on the wallpaper,
I haunt that room, I go into death in that room,
where my parents and my brother are.
It's quiet and cold but not scary.

The cold is pure and clean.
I'll go up there and watch the sun
until it disappears behind the rooftops.

Often a cat just outside my vision, sometimes moving under a tree or standing in the path. Sometimes only in a dream. The last one in the dream—she is limp and bleeding and I'm holding her to my chest and walking with her, We've been chased away and we are all the other one has. I don't weep and she is still but living. My arms are around her but the lower half of her swings a little as we go along and there are drops of blood on the ground. She is small but not a baby, animals are not babies to humans or should not be, should not be, that is important.

The cat is soft and gray. In my dream what is around me changes and doesn't matter. Under my feet the ground can tilt or floorboards can shake and splinter or space can open up. A dream has a purpose, through all the changes under my feet. This dream is about the feel of fur against skin. It is about shadows at the edge of the known world moving just out of sight and no one wants to see them. To each other we matter completely, to others not at all. This is safety in its own way, and the cat, who is an old female in the dream, is safe with me. The dream turns into a wave of desperate hope, I must keep her safe, as I wake into a dark morning.

Up on the third floor I opened a trunk and Schiaparelli's Shocking was in the room, Mother's perfume. I chose it for her at the department store where I worked for so many years.

I walked by the perfume counter in the department store every morning on my way to the elevator. The store was in half light and the crystal bottles gleamed on the glass counter and in the glass cabinets. Laura the perfume salesgirl dusted the bottles with a gray feather duster. She helped me choose Mother's perfume every birthday. For years it was Tweed, light and dry like October leaves. Then we found Shocking by Schiaparelli. Even when Mother got sick years later I put drops of Shocking on a linen handkerchief for her to hold.

Laura said to me once, "The Italian girls wear black skirts and white blouses, with a black jacket. You could just do that, you'd look smart, with your braid." I didn't like black and white. I wore what Mother called soft colors. And sweaters not jackets, more comfortable. I was a bookkeeper, I didn't have to wear short skirts and nipped-in jackets like Laura. I was good with numbers, Dad always said. He wanted me to be a CPA but I liked my job.

I still have most of the clothes I wore to work, I bought them in the best department of the store. Mother told me I'd never go wrong with Jaeger. I didn't buy more clothes after I stopped working. Mother needed me at home, first for Dad, then for herself. Joe came home and helped—I couldn't lift them and even when we had nurses there were times Joe had to lift them. Finally it was just Joe and me, and then he died, too.

Whenever the sun shines in our gray city, in whatever season, I think about desire. Desire is heat. Even terrible desires—to kill, to be avenged, to destroy, to shame, to conquer—bring blood to the surface of our skin, make us into columns of flame.

I am trying to imagine a cold desire on this cold winter afternoon, but even now, I'm warm—my cheeks, my chest, my thighs, filling with desire. I like the sensation. I give myself up to it. I no longer have the shaming desires that made me follow one person, then another, hardly seeing the object of desire but consumed—there it is, heat and fire—with the belief that I had to *have* the person. I never asked myself what the having might consist of or why I wanted it.

It was not love. Love was something given to me with no effort at all by Mother and Dad and Joe. I am sure I gave it back, I must have, I hope I did. I didn't notice it, but it flowed underground, cool and constant.

My mother and father died, one after the other. Then I was a cold river, a surface on which the sun never shone. Joe died, too. I felt jagged ice rushing through me—he died in the coldest January in years. Nothing melted. No heat to melt anything, the opposite of desire.

Years later I am filled with desire. I have learned that desire is in everything, and I desire everything I see around me. Desire is what makes tree branches beautiful. The branches are the expression of the tree's desire to grow. I am overcome by the crown of the bare maple trees in the park.

I'm wasting time sitting
in this shadowed room.
I want to go out to the park,
sit all night on the bench.
The night sky takes a long time,
it has a long story to tell
in these long nights.

Coat, scarf, hat, gloves, key.
I am out. I look up
at layers of fast gray clouds.
They break up, catch up, disappear.

The sky is black now, hard and clear
with winter stars like ice.
I can hold them, feel them
breaking up in my hands.

A sudden mist throws a net of water,
trapping light that shone
on other times.

I am glad I've stayed.
Here is the new winter moon,
a sharp blade on a circle of black glass.

It is past midnight,
bells rang long ago,
behind the moon a white fog
rolls in to cover the heavens.
No one here can penetrate
that secret part of the winter sky.
Other beings walk behind that curtain,
looking for other gods.

On winter days I sometimes sit out here in the snow. I can't sit in the rain, but I love the snow when it's dry, the big flakes coming down from gray clouds and the sun shining through the clouds in thin shafts. We went to the ballet when I was young, even my little brother Joe came along. The snow and the arms of the sun remind me of the dancers bending and fluttering and turning and lifting on the air. You have to wait for moments when glassy shards of sun pierce the thick rolling sky. It's hard weather but I have my old cashmere coat over sweaters, I have a woolen cap and lined rubber boots, brown suede gloves rubbed shiny, with a couple of holes showing the woolen lining, but still warm.

Some days I concentrate on the animals and the birds in the snow, the sparrows and chickadees and the family of crows. The crows are a different order of beings altogether, I can hear them arguing and warning, and I think they're talking about me, not exclusively but just in passing, though I'm not a threat. It's just that they patrol the neighborhood. I wish I could see it as they do.

It's early December, Christmas in the stores.
I'm small,
I look into the candy case head on.

There's the ribbon candy, so brittle,
twisting back on itself,
green and white,
pink and white,
red and white,
broad white center stripes
like slopes for fast sleds.
Not good to eat, you'll cut your tongue.

Next to the ribbons, the bon bons,
pale green and yellow and pink
easing open against your tongue
to the pure white coconut inside.

In this freezing Christmastime
the sweet shock of coconut,
from islands in warm seas.
Tahiti? Trinidad? I mix them up, but I know
the beaches are littered with brown coconuts,
the seas are striped purple and green and turquoise.

And the deserts: date palms in a desert oasis,
soft air stinging with blown grains of sand.
Coconuts, too, there must be coconut palms.
I see the three wise men, stopping at the oasis,
eating the fragrant white fruit, drinking the sweet juice.

My face presses against the glass.
Here, hidden under the pastel coatings, the coconut,
Here, inside the frilly paper,
the faraway taste, the ancient story,
waiting for us to break open the secret once again.

You learn how to be safe.
You learn not to go certain places.
I am safe with cats not dogs.
I am safe in the park not the downtown.
I am safe in the house.
I am safe alone not with people.
I was never safe with people
outside the house.
I know that now.

Mother and Dad never understood.
They said I was a beautiful girl--
such thick shiny hair.
But in the horrible notebooks
that went around the school
there was never anything but "OK"
beside my name, not even "nice."
One person, maybe two, wrote "bookworm."

I went away and I was lonely.
Girls taught me
to find boys, men they called them,
to be with, a lot of them. I counted them
but learned nothing from them.

Now at night I am batted around huge cities
and echoing rooms like mazes and puzzles.
I hide in stands of tall trees.
To come back to quiet is better, each morning
is better, and my fear
drains away into the whitening light.
Sometimes trails of half-remembered fear
snake around the edges
of where I walk and what I see all morning,
all day, and echoes of dropping off into nothing.

I was not betrayed by one man. I sparked like a box full of matches and burned out. I did not lose a great love the way they said our Latin teacher did, in the war. Everyone said she drank. I had no great romance, though like her I drank a lot. I could open to a man without desire and without satisfaction. Nothing in my young life prepared me for being opened like that, hollowed out, the self annihilated by desperation. Going home from the great cities of my desire, New York and Washington and Baltimore, for holidays, for summer. I was remote, a ghost walking through my childhood with fear and revulsion. Until I came home for good to our city that was not great, not seductive, not dangerous. Mother and Dad were cautious around me. We never mentioned the dresses I brought home from New York, or the times I called, crying, from Baltimore.

Cities are full of doorways.
In Baltimore and New York
I looked for doorways
that led down out of the cold
      into
            cellars
and if I was lucky
      into
            labyrinths.

I looked for smoky rooms
      perfumed with desire, animal smells
            not flowers or fruits.

I remember a place with lamps on tables
      casting rose light,
      and the fumes of whiskey
            sharp and delicious
            and music that warmed like whiskey.

In those rooms I looked for people
who lived in the night,
      had a look of mystery about them,
            I wanted to follow them through doorways
                down and farther down.
      I was half-blinded by desires I couldn't name.

I wanted to be anointed,
      received into secrets and mysteries.
I wanted priests and priestesses,
      and if priests were cruel I believed
      the cruelty was the rite.

When I woke flayed and shamed at first light
      I swept up bits of myself like
      tatters of ceremonial robes.

IV. Spring

Walking out into afternoons
my feet so light
time obliterated
no after no before.

In spring sunlight
is high and brittle,
in summer hissing and sparking,
in autumn pouring over my hands.

A spring afternoon,
wide empty streets.
Sun annihilates movement
and sound,
I walk into stillness,
to meet myself,
I am trapped by air, sun, silence.

then the silence is broken,
a distant wind howling behind the
shimmer of the lighted landscape
a disappearance of time
no after no before
maybe on this spring walk, at the horizon,
I will no longer feel my feet beneath me.

My friend Miss Roxanne has diabetes. She's tried to watch her sugar, but it's caught up with her, she couldn't fool it. Diabetes and the high blood pressure too. Runs in the family. But what does not run in her family is Oldtimers Disease. She laughed and laughed about that, Oldtimers Disease. I laughed too, but then we were both quiet because it is the one thing we fear, the heavy fog we can almost feel descending on us as we sit on the bench.. We don't admit it out loud to each other, we just walk up to it, the dark edge of it, and then we're quiet. That's how we tell each other how afraid we are. Words are sometimes just noise to hold up against fear. Miss Roxanne and I are often quiet together, because we aren't afraid of much. But she has told me her mother is ninety-six and sharp as a tack, and her grandmother lived to a hundred and remembered the names and birthdays of every single member of her family, which was more than a hundred people. Those are the numbers she holds up against her fear, ninety-six and a hundred. Your people died younger than that, she says to me, but I tell you, Miss Margaret, you are doing fine and better than fine, you have nothing to worry about. Roxanne knows some people think I'm crazy or senile or both. I once started to ask her,

      Do you think I . . . ?

and she waved her hand to tell me to be quiet. We doing fine, we doing better than fine, she said.

Today was cold and overcast, a sort of weather I have come to love. It was a day of crows. They were mad, screaming all over the sky, all day, lighting in the trees of the park, one, then another, legs held under them neatly, as if they might pick up offerings from the ground. Their immense wings were violent and intemperate, like their chorus of raw speech. Why do I know nothing about them, whether it was the season that sent them into their wild performance, or the weather, or an enemy, or a ritual of their own, something to do with celebration, or competition? I've never heard or read anything about crows being happy. Exultant, maybe. But why should all those wheelings and callings not be about happiness? They were so close to me, falling and gliding from above the trees and houses. I stood up from the bench and turned and turned, my neck craning until it hurt, to follow the spectacle. That was early in the day, and again in the afternoon when I came back out. Finally, I checked the park at dusk, and they were gone. The heavy gray mass of cloud had lifted. The sky was lighted blue-black but clear. It was a moment I was glad to see: so many, now, like that. They are each one first, and last, or might be. I live finally in a turning sphere, moving only in a perfect cycle through the seasons.

MADBOOKS

Senior Editor: Jan Beatty

Poetry Editor: Martha Ruschman

Assistant Editors: Lisa Alexander, Kayla Sargeson

Design: Todd Sanders - www.locusgraphic.com